The Drivers
Advanced Quiz Book

THE BOOK

This book has been prepared to help 21st century drivers improve their road skills and their theory of driving. It follows closely the rules and regulations for safe driving as laid down by the Driving & Vehicle Standards Agency (DVSA). It contains 350 multiple choice questions, complete with answers, in seven banks of 50 questions each. The correct answers are shown at the end of each bank of questions.

   This book will enable you to become a better and therefore safer driver. It costs about the same as a couple of cups of coffee which is a bargain by any standard for worry free motoring.

Copyright © James Duggan – 17th April 2019

THE AUTHOR

Jim has spent many years in the driver training business, both as a first class driving instructor and latterly involved in the training of instructors with the publication of driver training aids and manuals.

With a pass rate of 78% when the general pass rate was only 32% he has a proven track record which served his pupils well. Having driven over an estimated two million miles he has a wealth of knowledge to pass on to both learners and experienced drivers. As he has now retired from the practical side of the business he wants to pass on all that know-how to anyone who may benefit from it.

All versions of his driver training series can be obtained via the Amazon Kindle Book Store at – **www.amazon.co.uk**.

CONTENTS

Page

QUESTION BANK – A

1. **You are travelling behind a bus which pulls up at a bus stop. What would you do?** (TWO answers)

    a. Accelerate past the bus sounding your horn.
    b. Watch carefully for pedestrians.
    c. Be ready to give way to the bus.
    d. Pull in closely behind the bus.

2. **Why is coasting wrong?**

    a. It will cause the car to skid.
    b. It will make the engine stall.
    c. The engine will run faster.

3. **Give TWO reasons for using an additive in the windscreen washer reservoir.**

    a. To prevent freezing in winter.
    b. To wipe off leaves in autumn.
    c. To help prevent mould growth.
    d. To clear dead insects in summer.
    e. To prevent corrosion.

4. **You have to make a journey in foggy conditions. You should**

    a. Follow closely the tail lights of other vehicles.
    b. Never use demisters and windscreen wipers.
    c. Leave plenty of time for your journey.
    d. Keep two seconds behind other vehicles.

5. **You have just passed your driving test. How likely are you to have an accident compared with other drivers?**

    a. More likely.
    b. It depends on your age.
    c. Less likely.
    d. About the same.

6. **The road is wet. Why might a motorcyclist steer round drain covers on a bend?**

    a. To avoid puncturing tyres on the edges of drain covers.
    b. To prevent the motorcycle sliding on the metal drain covers.
    c. To help judge bends using drain covers as markers.
    d. To avoid splashing pedestrians on the pavement.

7. A car driver pulls out causing you to brake. You should

   a. Keep calm and not retaliate.
   b. Overtake and sound your horn.
   c. Drive closely behind and sound your horn.
   d. Flag the driver down and explain the mistake.

8. You are driving in town. There is a bus at the bus stop on the other side of the road. Why should you be careful?

   a. The bus may have broken down.
   b. Pedestrians may come from behind the bus.
   c. The bus may move off suddenly.
   d. The bus may remain stationary.

9. Your car has third party insurance. What does this cover? (THREE answers)

   a. Damage to your own car.
   b. Damage to your car by fire.
   c. Injury to another person.
   d. Damage to another persons' property.
   e. Damage to other vehicles.
   f. Injury to yourself.

10. Which of the following are hazards motorcyclists present in queues of traffic? (THREE answers)

   a. Cutting in just in front of you.
   b. Riding in single file.
   c. Passing very close to your car.
   d. Riding with their headlamp on dipped beam.
   e. Filtering between the lanes.

11. How can you best control your vehicle when driving in snow?

   a. By driving slowly in as high a gear as possible.
   b. By staying in low gear and gripping the steering wheel tightly.
   c. By driving in first gear.
   d. By keeping engine revs high and slipping the clutch.

12. Your car is fitted with child safety door locks. When used this means that normally

   a. The rear doors can only be opened from the outside.
   b. The rear doors can only be opened from the inside.
   c. All the doors can only be opened from the outside.
   d. All the doors can only be opened from the inside.

13. Your driving licence must be signed by

   a. A police officer.
   b. A driving instructor.
   c. Your next of kin.
   d. You.

14. A driver attends a social event. What precaution should the driver take?

   a. Drink plenty of coffee after drinking alcohol.
   b. Avoid busy roads after drinking alcohol.
   c. Avoid drinking alcohol completely.
   d. Avoid drinking alcohol on an empty stomach.

15. At a railway level crossing the red light signal continues to flash after the train has gone by. What should you do?

   a. Phone the signal operator.
   b. Alert drivers behind you.
   c. Wait.
   d. Proceed with caution.

16. How should you drive around a bend on ice?

   a. Using the clutch and brake together.
   b. In first gear.
   c. Braking as you enter the bend.
   d. Slowly and smoothly.

17. You are driving in poor visibility. You can see more than 100 metres (330 feet) ahead. How can you make sure that other vehicles can see you?

   a. Turn on your dipped headlights.
   b. Follow the vehicle in front closely.
   c. Turn on your rear fog lights.
   d. Keep well out towards the middle of the road.

18. What is the most common factor in causing road accidents?

   a. Weather conditions.
   b. Driver error.
   c. Road conditions.
   d. Mechanical failure.

19. When you are overtaking a cyclist you should leave as much room as you would give a car. Why is this?

    a.   The cyclist might change lanes.
    b.   The cyclist might get off the bike.
    c.   The cyclist might swerve.
    d.   The cyclist might have to make a right turn.

20. You have taken medication which may make you drowsy. Your friends tell you it is safe to drive. What should you do?

    a.   Take their advice and drive.
    b.   Ignore their advice and do not drive.
    c.   Only drive if they come with you.
    d.   Drive for short distances only.

21. How will a school crossing patrol signal you to stop?

    a.   By pointing to children on the opposite pavement.
    b.   By displaying a red light.
    c.   By displaying a stop sign.
    d.   By giving you an arm signal.

22. A police officer asks to see your driving documents. You do not have them with you. You may produce them at a police station within

    a.   5 Days.
    b.   7 Days.
    c.   14 Days.
    d.   21 Days.

23. At road junctions, which of the following are most vulnerable? (THREE answers)

    a.   Cyclists.
    b.   Motorcyclists.
    c.   Pedestrians.
    d.   Car drivers.
    e.   Lorry drivers.

24. You are going straight ahead at a roundabout. How should you signal?

    a.   Signal right on the approach and then left to leave the roundabout.
    b.   Signal left as you leave the roundabout.
    c.   Signal left on the approach and keep the signal on until you leave.
    d.   Signal left just as you pass the exit before the one you will take.

25. For which THREE should you use your hazard warning lights?

    a. When you are parking in a restricted area.
    b. When you are temporarily obstructing traffic.
    c. To warn following traffic of a hazard ahead.
    d. When you have broken down.

26. Motorcycle riders are vulnerable because they

    a. Are easy for other road users to see.
    b. Are difficult for other road users to see.
    c. Are more likely to break down.
    d. Cannot give arm signals.

27. Your overall stopping distance will be much longer when driving

    a. In the rain.
    b. In fog.
    c. At night.
    d. In strong winds.

28. A car driver must ensure that seat belts are worn by

    a. All front seat passengers.
    b. All passengers.
    c. All rear seat passengers.
    d. Children under 14 years old.

29. What is the maximum speed limit on a single carriageway road?

    a. 50 mph.
    b. 60 mph.
    c. 40 mph.
    d. 70 mph.

30. Motor cars and motor cycles must first have an M.O.T. certificate when they are

    a. One year old.
    b. Three years old.
    c. Five years old.
    d. Seven years old.

31. You are driving past parked cars. You notice the wheel of a bicycle sticking out between them. What should you do?

   a. Accelerate past quickly and sound your horn.
   b. Slow down and wave the cyclist across.
   c. Brake sharply and flash your headlights.
   d. Slow down and be prepared to stop for a cyclist.

32. You are driving on a motorway. Red flashing lights appear above your lane. What should you do?

   a. Continue in that lane and await further information.
   b. Go no further in that lane.
   c. Drive onto the hard shoulder.
   d. Stop and wait for an instruction to proceed.

33. What must a driver do at a pelican crossing when the amber light is flashing?

   a. Signal the pedestrian to cross.
   b. Always wait for the green light before proceeding.
   c. Give way to any pedestrians on the crossing.
   d. Wait for the red and amber light before proceeding.

34. You are approaching a bend at speed. You should begin to brake

   a. On the bend.
   b. After the bend.
   c. After changing gears.
   d. Before the bend.

35. Whilst driving, a warning light on your instrument panel comes on. What should you do?

   a. Continue if the engine sounds all right.
   b. Hope that it is just a temporary electrical fault.
   c. Deal with the problem when there is more time.
   d. Check out the problem quickly and safely.

36. You arrive at the scene of a motorcycle accident. No other vehicle is involved. The rider is unconscious and lying in the middle of the road. The first thing you should do is

   a. Move the rider out of the road.
   b. Warn other traffic.
   c. Clear the road of debris.
   d. Give the rider reassurance.

37. You are carrying two children and their parents in your car. Who is responsible for seeing that the children wear seat belts?

    a. The children's parents.
    b. You.
    c. The front seat passenger.
    d. The children.

38. You are not sure if your cough medicine will affect your driving. What TWO things could you do?

    a. Ask your doctor.
    b. Check the medicine label.
    c. Drive if you feel all right.
    d. Ask a friend or relative for advice.

39. There is a tractor ahead of you. You wish to overtake, but are not sure if it is safe to do so. You should

    a. Follow another overtaking vehicle through.
    b. Sound your horn for the slow vehicle to pull over.
    c. Speed through, but flash your lights to oncoming traffic.
    d. Not overtake if you are in doubt.

40. In which TWO places must you not park?

    a. Near a school entrance.
    b. Near a police station.
    c. In a side road.
    d. At a bus stop.
    e. In a one way street.

41. Where would you see a contra-flow bus and cycle lane?

    a. On a dual carriageway.
    b. On a roundabout.
    c. On an urban motorway.
    d. On a one way street.

42. You are approaching a busy junction. There are several lanes with road markings. At the last moment you realise that you are in the wrong lane. You should

    a. Continue in that lane.
    b. Force your way across.
    c. Stop until the area has cleared.
    d. Use clear arm signals to cut across.

43. When motorists flash their headlights at you it means

    a. That there is a radar speed trap ahead.
    b. That they are giving way to you.
    c. That they are warning you of their presence.
    d. That there is something wrong with your vehicle.

44. You are towing a trailer on a motorway. What is your maximum speed limit?

    a. 40mph.
    b. 50mph.
    c. 60mph.
    d. 70mph.

45. When driving towards a bright setting sun, glare can be reduced by

    a. Closing one eye.
    b. Dipping the interior mirror.
    c. Wearing dark glasses.
    d. Looking sideways.

46. Whilst driving you approach road works. You see a temporary maximum speed limit sign. You must

    a. Comply with the sign during the working day.
    b. Comply with the sign at all times.
    c. Comply with the sign when the lanes are narrow.
    d. Comply with the sign during the hours of darkness.

47. Why should you make sure that you have cancelled your indicators after turning?

    a. To avoid flattening the battery.
    b. To avoid misleading other road users.
    c. To avoid dazzling other road users.
    d. To avoid damage to the indicator relay.

48. You are driving on a wet motorway with surface spray. You should

    a. Use your hazard flashers.
    b. Use dipped headlights.
    c. Use your rear fog lights.
    d. Drive in any lane which has no traffic.

49. At toucan crossings, apart from pedestrians you should be aware of

    a. Emergency vehicles emerging.
    b. Buses pulling out.
    c. Trams crossing in front.
    d. Cyclists riding across.

50. You break down on a level crossing. The lights have not yet begun to flash. Which THREE things should you do?

    a. Telephone the signal operator.
    b. Leave your vehicle and get everyone clear.
    c. Walk down the track to signal the next train.
    d. Move the vehicle if the signal operator tells you to.
    e. Tell drivers behind what has happened.

ANSWERS QUESTION BANK – A

1bc   2d   3ad   4c   5a   6b   7a   8b   9cde   10ace   11a   12a   13d   14c

15c   16d   17a   18b   19c   20b   21c   22b   23abc   24d   25bcd   26b

27a   28b   29b   30b   31d   32b   33c   34d   35d   36b   37b   38ab   39d

40ad   41d   42a   43c   44c   45c   46b   47b   48b   49d   50abd

1. In which THREE of these situations may you overtake another vehicle on the left?

    a. When you are in a one-way street.
    b. When approaching a motorway slip road where you will be turning off.
    c. When the vehicle in front is signalling to turn right.
    d. When a slower vehicle is travelling in the right hand lane of a dual carriageway.
    e. In slow moving traffic queues when traffic in the right hand lane is moving more slowly.

2. You are driving in very wet weather. Your vehicle begins to slide. This effect is called

    a. Hosing.
    b. Weaving.
    c. Aquaplaning.
    d. Fading.

3. You should switch your rear fog lights on when visibility drops below

    a. Your overall stopping distance.
    b. Ten car lengths.
    c. 10 metres. (33 feet)
    d. 100 metres. (330 feet)

4. Which age group is most likely to be involved in a road accident?

    a. 36 to 45 year olds.
    b. 55 year olds and over.
    c. 46 to 55 year olds.
    d. 17 to 25 year olds.

5. You keep well back whilst waiting to overtake a large vehicle. Another car fills the gap. You should

    a. Sound your horn.
    b. Drop back further.
    c. Flash your headlights.
    d. Start to overtake.

6. To correct a rear wheel skid you should

   a. Not turn at all.
   b. Turn away from it.
   c. Turn into it.
   d. Apply your handbrake.

7. You are driving in fog. Why should you keep well back from the vehicle in front?

   a. In case it changes direction suddenly.
   b. In case its' fog lights dazzle you.
   c. In case it stops suddenly.
   d. In case its' brake lights dazzle you.

8. Why should you always reduce your speed when driving in fog?

   a. Because the brakes do not work as well.
   b. Because you could be dazzled by the fog lights of other vehicles.
   c. Because the engine is colder.
   d. Because it is more difficult to see events ahead.

9. Freezing conditions will affect the distance it takes you to come to a stop. You should expect stopping distances to increase by up to

   a. Two times.
   b. Five times.
   c. Three times.
   d. Ten times.

10. If you notice a strong smell of petrol as you drive along you should

    a. Not worry as it is only exhaust fumes.
    b. Carry on at a reduced speed.
    c. Expect it to stop in a few miles.
    d. Stop and investigate the problem.

11. The right hand lane of a three lane motorway is

    a. For lorries only.
    b. An overtaking lane.
    c. The right turn lane.
    d. An acceleration lane.

12. A pedestrian steps out into the road just ahead of you. What should you do first?

    a. Sound your horn.
    b. Check your mirror.
    c. Flash your headlights.
    d. Press the brake.

13. You are towing a vehicle and experience snaking. How would you reduce it?

    a. Ease off the accelerator slowly.
    b. Press the accelerator firmly.
    c. Steer sharply.
    d. Brake hard.

14. You should only use rear fog lights when you cannot see further than about

    a. 100 metres (330 feet).
    b. 200 metres (660 feet).
    c. 250 metres (800 feet).
    d. 150 metres (495 feet).

15. Which TWO things should you do when a front tyre bursts?

    a. Apply the handbrake to stop the vehicle.
    b. Brake firmly and quickly.
    c. Let the vehicle roll to a stop.
    d. Hold the steering wheel lightly.
    e. Grip the steering wheel firmly.

16. On a motorway the hard shoulder should be used

    a. To answer a mobile phone.
    b. When an emergency arises.
    c. For a short rest when tired.
    d. To check a road atlas.

17. You wish to overtake on a dual carriageway. You see in your mirror that the car behind has pulled out to overtake you. You should

    a. Not signal until the car has passed.
    b. Signal and pull out to overtake.
    c. Signal to tell the driver behind that you also want to overtake.
    d. Touch the brakes to show your brake lights.

18. Your vehicle is parked on the road at night. When must you use side lights?

   a. Where there are continuous white lines in the middle of the road.
   b. Where the speed limit exceeds 30 mph.
   c. Where you are facing on-coming traffic.
   d. Where you are near a bus stop.

19. Which THREE should you do when passing sheep on the road?

   a. Allow plenty of room.
   b. Drive very slowly.
   c. Pass quickly, but quietly.
   d. Briefly sound your horn.
   e. Be ready to stop.

20. What is the legal minimum insurance cover you must have to drive on a public road?

   a. Third party, fire and theft.
   b. Fully comprehensive.
   c. Third party only.
   d. Personal injury cover.

21. When traffic lights are out of order, who has priority?

   a. Traffic going straight on.
   b. Traffic turning right.
   c. Nobody.
   d. Traffic turning left.

22. What is the shortest stopping distance on a dry road from 60mph?

   a. 53 metres. (175 feet)
   b. 58 metres. (190 feet)
   c. 73 metres. (240 feet)
   d. 96 metres. (315 feet)

23. You are driving on a road which has a cycle lane. The lane is marked by a solid white line. This means

   a. You must not drive in the lane unless unavoidable.
   b. The lane can be used for parking your vehicle.
   c. You can drive in the lane at any time.
   d. The lane must be used by motorcycles in heavy traffic.

24. When following a large vehicle you must keep well back because

    a. It allows the driver to see you in his mirrors.
    b. It helps the large vehicle to stop more easily.
    c. It allows you to corner more quickly.
    d. It helps you to keep out of the wind.

25. You are driving in fog. The vehicle behind seems to be very close. You should

    a. Switch on your hazard warning lights.
    b. Pull over and stop immediately.
    c. Speed up to get away.
    d. Continue cautiously.

26. Which of these vehicles is least likely to be affected by crosswinds?

    a. Cyclists.
    b. Motorcyclists.
    c. High sided vehicles.
    d. Cars.

27. If you are feeling tired it is best to stop as soon as you can. Until then you should

    a. Increase your speed to find a stopping place quickly.
    b. Ensure a supply of fresh air.
    c. Gently tap the steering wheel.
    d. Keep changing speed to improve concentration.

28. You may drive on a footpath

    a. To overtake slow moving traffic.
    b. When the pavement is very wide.
    c. If no pedestrians are near.
    d. To get into property.

29. You want to turn right from a main road into a side road. Just before turning you should

    a. Cancel your right turn signal.
    b. Select first gear.
    c. Check for traffic overtaking on your right.
    d. Stop and set the hand brake.

30. **You have broken down on a motorway. When you use the emergency telephone you will be asked** (THREE answers)

    a.   For the number on the telephone you are using.
    b.   For your driving licence details.
    c.   For the name of your vehicle insurance company.
    d.   For details of yourself and your vehicle.
    e.   Whether you belong to a motoring organisation.

31. **Which of these vehicles is not required to have an M.O.T. certificate?** (THREE answers)

    a.   Police vehicle.
    b.   Small trailer.
    c.   Ambulance.
    d.   Taxi.
    e.   Caravan.

32. **What does 'tailgating' mean?**

    a.   When a vehicle delivering goods has its' tailgate down.
    b.   When a vehicle is travelling with its' back doors open.
    c.   When a driver is following another vehicle too closely
    d.   When stationary vehicles are too close in a queue.

33. **Which THREE of the following do you need to have before you can drive legally?**

    a.   A valid signed driving licence.
    b.   A valid tax disc displayed on your vehicle.
    c.   Proof of your identity.
    d.   A current M.O.T. certificate if the car is over three years old (four years in Northern Ireland).
    e.   Fully comprehensive insurance.
    f.   A vehicle handbook.

34. **Stopping in good conditions at 30 mph takes at least**

    a.   Two car lengths.
    b.   Six car lengths.
    c.   Three car lengths.
    d.   One car length.

35. Which vehicle may have to use a different course to normal at roundabouts?

    a. A sports car.
    b. A van.
    c. An estate car.
    d. A long vehicle.

36. What is the shortest stopping distance at 70mph?

    a. 53 metres (175 feet).
    b. 60 metres (200 feet).
    c. 73 metres (240 feet).
    d. 96 metres (315 feet).

37. You are driving on a motorway. You have to slow down quickly due to a hazard. You should

    a. Switch on your hazard lights.
    b. Switch on your headlights.
    c. Sound your horn.
    d. Flash your headlights.

38. How will a police officer in a patrol car get you to stop?

    a. Flash his headlights indicate left and point to the left.
    b. Wait until you stop and then approach you.
    c. Use the siren, overtake and cut in front and stop.
    d. Pull alongside you, use the siren and wave you to stop.

39. What will cause high fuel consumption?

    a. Poor steering control.
    b. Accelerating around bends.
    c. Driving in high gears.
    d. Harsh braking and acceleration.

40. On a three lane motorway, which lane should you use for normal driving?

    a. Left.
    b. Right.
    c. Centre.
    d. Either the right or centre.

41. You should never attempt to overtake a cyclist

    a. Just before you turn left.
    b. Just before you turn right.
    c. On a one way street.
    d. On a dual carriageway.

42. What colour are the reflective studs between the main carriageway and the slip road on a motorway?

    a. Amber.
    b. White.
    c. Green.
    d. Red.

43. When may you stop on a motorway? (THREE answers)

    a. If you have to read a map.
    b. When you are tired and need a rest.
    c. If red lights show above your lane.
    d. When told to do so by the police.
    e. If a child in the car feels ill.
    f. In an emergency or breakdown.

44. You are on a motorway. Luggage falls from your vehicle. What should you do?

    a. Stop at the next emergency telephone and contact the police.
    b. Stop on the motorway and put on your hazard lights whilst you pick it up.
    c. Reverse back up the motorway and pick it up.
    d. Pull up on the hard shoulder and wave traffic down.

45. You are driving at the legal speed limit. A vehicle comes up quickly behind you flashing its' headlights. You should

    a. Accelerate to maintain a gap behind you.
    b. Touch the brakes to show your brake lights.
    c. Maintain your speed and prevent the vehicle from overtaking.
    d. Allow the vehicle to overtake.

46. Braking distances on ice can be

    a. Twice the normal distance.
    b. Five times the normal distance.
    c. Seven times the normal distance.
    d. Ten times the normal distance.

47. **You may remove your seat belts when carrying out a manoeuvre which involves**

 a. Reversing.
 b. A hill start.
 c. An emergency stop.
 d. Driving slowly.

48. **When should you beckon pedestrians to cross the road?**

 a. At pedestrian crossings.
 b. At no time.
 c. At junctions.
 d. At school crossings.

49. **You are following other vehicles in fog with your lights on. How else can you reduce the chances of being involved in an accident?**

 a. Keep close to the vehicle in front.
 b. Use your main beams instead of dipped headlights.
 c. Keep together with the faster vehicles.
 d. Reduce your speed and increase the gap between you and the vehicle in front.

50. **Whilst driving the fog clears and you can see more clearly. You must remember to**

 a. Switch off the fog lights.
 b. Reduce your speed.
 c. Switch off the demister.
 d. Close any open windows.

ANSWERS QUESTION BANK – B

1ace 2c 3d 4d 5b 6c 7c 8d 9d 10d 11b 12d 13a 14a 15ce

16b 17a 18b 19abe 20c 21c 22c 23a 24a 25d 26d 27b 28d

29c 30ade 31be 32c 33abd 34b 35d 36d 37a 38a 39d 40a

41a 42c 43cdf 44a 45d 46d 47a 48b 49d 50a

QUESTION BANK – C

1. **When may you not overtake on the left?**

   a. On a free flowing motorway or dual carriageway.
   b. When the traffic is moving slowly in queues.
   c. On a one way street.
   d. When the car in front is signalling to turn right.

2. **At pelican crossings flashing amber means you should**

   a. Stop if you can do so safely.
   b. Give way to pedestrians already on the crossing.
   c. Stop and wait for the green light.
   d. Give way to pedestrians waiting to cross.

3. **When you cannot see clearly behind when reversing, what should you do?**

   a. Open your window to look behind.
   b. Open the door and look behind.
   c. Look through the nearside window.
   d. Ask someone to guide you.

4. **A friend wants to teach you to drive a car. They must**

   a. Be over 21 and have held a full licence for at least two years.
   b. Be over 18 and hold an advanced drivers' certificate.
   c. Be over 18 and have fully comprehensive insurance.
   d. Be over 21 and have held a full licence for at least three years.

5. **Another driver does something which upsets you. You should**

   a. Try not to react.
   b. Let them know how you feel.
   c. Flash your headlights several times.
   d. Sound your horn.

6. **You are driving a vehicle fitted with a hand held telephone. To answer the telephone you must**

   a. Find a safe place to stop.
   b. Reduce your speed.
   c. Steer the car with one hand.
   d. Be particularly careful at junctions.

7. Which THREE of the following will affect your overall stopping distance?

   a. How fast you are going.
   b. The tyres on your vehicle.
   c. The time of day.
   d. The weather.
   e. The street lighting.

8. Before driving another persons' motor vehicle you should make sure that

   a. The vehicle owner has third party insurance cover.
   b. Your own vehicle has insurance cover.
   c. The vehicle is insured for your use.
   d. The owner has left the insurance documents in the vehicle.

9. On which THREE occasions must you stop your vehicle?

   a. When involved in an accident.
   b. At a red traffic light.
   c. When signalled to do so by a police officer.
   d. At a junction with double broken white lines.
   e. At a pelican crossing when the amber light is flashing and no pedestrians are crossing.

10. It is very windy. You are behind a motorcyclist who is overtaking a high sided vehicle. What should you do?

    a. Overtake the motorcyclist immediately.
    b. Keep well back.
    c. Stay level with the motorcyclist.
    d. Keep close to the motorcyclist.

11. You wish to overtake a long slow moving vehicle on a busy road. You should

    a. Wait behind until the driver waves you past.
    b. Flash your lights for the oncoming traffic to give way.
    c. Follow closely whilst moving out to see the road ahead.
    d. Keep well back until you can see that it is clear.

12. For which TWO should you use hazard warning lights?

    a. When you slow down quickly on a motorway because of a hazard ahead.
    b. When you have broken down.
    c. When you wish to stop on double yellow lines.
    d. When you need to park on the pavement.

13. What do child locks on a vehicle do?

    a. Lock the seat belt buckles in place.
    b. Lock the rear windows in the up position.
    c. Stop children from opening the rear doors.
    d. Stop the rear seats from tipping forward.

14. In an accident whilst driving someone is injured. You do not have the insurance certificate at the time. You must report it to the police as soon as possible or in any case within

    a. 24 hours.
    b. 48 hours.
    c. Five days.
    d. Seven days.

15. Your vehicle needs a current M.O.T. certificate. You do not have one. Until you do you will not be able to renew your

    a. Driving licence.
    b. Vehicle insurance.
    c. Road tax disc.
    d. Vehicle registration document.

16. When your vehicle is loaded you must make sure that the load will

    a. Remain secure.
    b. Be easy to unload.
    c. Not be damaged.
    d. Not damage the vehicle.

17. You are driving on a well lit motorway at night. You must

    a. Use only your side lights.
    b. Always use your headlights.
    c. Always use rear fog lights.
    d. Use headlights only in bad weather.

18. Are passengers allowed to ride in a caravan being towed?

    a. Yes.
    b. No.
    c. Only if all the seats in the towing vehicle are full.
    d. Only if a stabilizer is fitted.

19. You want to turn right at a box junction. You should

    a. Wait in the box junction until your exit is clear.
    b. Wait before the junction until clear of all traffic.
    c. Drive on. You cannot turn right at a box junction.
    d. Drive slowly into the box junction when signalled by oncoming traffic.

20. If a trailer swerves or snakes when being towed you should

    a. Ease off the accelerator and reduce your speed.
    b. Let the steering wheel go and let it correct itself.
    c. Brake hard and hold the pedal down.
    d. Increase your speed as quickly as possible.

21. You are involved in a road accident with another driver. Your vehicle is damaged. Which FOUR of the following should you find out?

    a. Whether the driver owns the other vehicle involved.
    b. The other drivers' name, address and telephone number.
    c. The make and registration number of the other vehicle.
    d. The occupation of the other driver.
    e. The details of the other drivers' vehicle insurance.
    f. Whether the other driver is licensed to drive.

22. Which FOUR of these must not use motorways?

    a. Learner car drivers.
    b. Motorcycles over 50 cc.
    c. Double-decker busses.
    d. Farm tractors.
    e. Horse riders.
    f. Cyclists.

23. At pelican crossings. What does the amber flashing light mean?

    a. You must not move off until the lights stop flashing.
    b. You must give way to pedestrians still on the crossing.
    c. You can move off even if pedestrians are still crossing.
    d. You must stop as the lights are about to change to red.

24. You arrive at the scene of a motorcycle accident. The rider is conscious, but in shock. You should make sure that

a. The riders' helmet is removed.
b. The rider is moved to the side of the road.
c. The riders' helmet is not removed.
d. The rider is put in the recovery position.

25. You are driving behind two cyclists. They approach a roundabout in the left hand lane. In which direction should you expect the cyclist to go?

a. Left.
b. Right.
c. Any direction.
d. Straight ahead.

26. How would you react to drivers who appear inexperienced?

a. Sound your horn to warn them of your presence.
b. Be patient and prepared for them to react more slowly.
c. Flash your headlights to indicate that it is safe for them to proceed.
d. Overtake them as soon as possible.

27. What TWO safeguards could you take against fire risk in your vehicle?

a. Keep water levels above the maximum.
b. Carry a fire extinguisher.
c. Avoid driving with a full tank of petrol.
d. Use unleaded petrol.
e. Check out any strong smell of petrol.
f. Use low octane fuel.

28. When driving in icy conditions the steering becomes light because the tyres

a. Have more grip on the road.
b. Are too soft.
c. Are too hard.
d. Have less grip on the road.

29. You should load a trailer so that the weight is

a. Mostly over the nearside wheel.
b. Evenly distributed.
c. Mainly at the front.
d. Mostly at the rear.

30. You are driving downhill. There is a car parked on the other side of the road. Large slow moving lorries are coming towards you. You should

    a. Keep going because you have right of way.
    b. Slow down and give way.
    c. Speed up and get past quickly.
    d. Pull over on the right behind the parked car.

31. In windy conditions you have to take extra care when

    a. Using the brakes.
    b. Making a hill start.
    c. Turning into a narrow road.
    d. Passing pedal cyclists.

32. When driving in snow it is best to keep in as high a gear as possible. Why is this?

    a. To help you slow down quickly when you brake.
    b. So that wheel spin does not cause the engine to run too fast.
    c. To leave a lower gear available in case of wheel spin.
    d. To help prevent wheel spin.

33. Your indicators may be difficult to see in bright sunlight. What should you do?

    a. Put your indicator on earlier.
    b. Give an arm signal as well as using your indicator.
    c. Touch the brake several times to show the stop lights.
    d. Turn as quickly as you can.

34. What will reduce the risk of neck injury in a collision?

    a. An air sprung seat.
    b. Antilock brakes.
    c. A collapsible steering wheel.
    d. A properly adjusted head restraint.

35. When following a motorcyclist on an uneven road you should

    a. Allow less room to be sure you can be seen in their mirrors.
    b. Overtake immediately.
    c. Allow extra room in case they swerve to miss potholes.
    d. Allow the same room as normal because motorcyclists are not affected by road surfaces.

36. You are driving along a street with parked vehicles on the left hand side. For which THREE reasons must you keep your speed down?

   a. So that oncoming traffic can see you more clearly.
   b. You may set off car alarms.
   c. Vehicles may be pulling out.
   d. Drivers' doors may open.
   e. Children may run out from between the vehicles.

37. You are driving at night. Why should you be extra careful of your speed?

   a. Because you might need to stop within the distance you can see to be clear.
   b. Because it uses more petrol.
   c. Because driving with lights on runs down the battery.
   d. Because you may be late.

38. You want to turn right at a junction, but you think that your indicators cannot be seen clearly. What should you do?

   a. Get out and check if the indicators can be seen.
   b. Stay in the left hand lane.
   c. Keep well over to the right.
   d. Give an arm signal as well as the indicator signal.

39. You have stopped at a pedestrian crossing to allow pedestrians to cross. You should

   a. Wait until they have crossed.
   b. Edge your vehicle forward slowly.
   c. Wait, revving your engine.
   d. Signal to pedestrians to cross.

40. You are in a one way street and want to turn right. You should position your vehicle

   a. In the right hand lane.
   b. In the left hand lane.
   c. In either lane depending on the traffic.
   d. Just left of the centre line.

41. You must stop when signalled to do so by which THREE of these?

   a. A police officer.
   b. A pedestrian.
   c. A school crossing patrol.
   d. A bus driver.
   e. A red traffic light.

42. When may you reverse from a side road into a main road?

   a. Only if both roads are clear of traffic.
   b. Not at any time.
   c. At any time.
   d. Only if the main road is clear of traffic.

43. You see a vehicle coming towards you on a single track road. You should

   a. Stop at a passing place.
   b. Reverse back to a main road.
   c. Do an emergency stop.
   d. Put on your hazard lights.

44. Car passengers must wear a seat belt if one is available unless they are

   a. Under 14 years old.
   b. Under 1.5 metres (5 feet) in height.
   c. Sitting in the rear seat.
   d. Exempt for medical reasons.

45. You are following a vehicle on a wet road. You should leave a time gap of at least

   a. One second.
   b. Two seconds.
   c. Three seconds.
   d. Four seconds.

46. You are driving on a three lane motorway at 70mph. There is no traffic ahead. Which lane should you use?

   a. Any lane.
   b. Middle lane.
   c. Right lane.
   d. Left lane.

47. Signals are normally given by direction indicators and

    a. Brake lights.
    b. Side lights.
    c. Fog lights.
    d. Interior lights.

48. Where may you overtake on a one way street?

    a. Only on the left hand side.
    b. Overtaking is not allowed.
    c. Only on the right hand side.
    d. Either on the right or the left.

49. You are driving in freezing conditions. What should you do when approaching a sharp left hand bend? (TWO answers)

    a. Slow down before you reach the bend.
    b. Gently apply the handbrake.
    c. Firmly use your footbrake.
    d. Coast into the bend.
    e. Avoid sudden steering movements.

50. Driving with under inflated tyres can affect (TWO answers)

    a. Engine temperature.
    b. Fuel consumption.
    c. Braking.
    d. Oil pressure.

ANSWERS QUESTION BANK – C

1a 2b 3d 4d 5a 6a 7abd 8c 9abc 10b 11d 12ab 13c 14a

15c 16a 17b 18b 19a 20a 21abce 22adef 23b 24c 25c 26b

27be 28d 29b 30b 31d 32d 33b 34d 35c 36cde 37a 38d

39a 40a 41ace 42b 43a 44d 45d 46d 47a 48d 49ae 50bc

QUESTION BANK – D

1. You have stopped at the scene of an accident to give help. Which THREE things should you do?

   a. Keep injured people warm and comfortable.
   b. Keep injured people calm, talking to them reassuringly.
   c. Keep injured people on the move by walking them around.
   d. Give injured people a warm drink.
   e. Make sure that injured people are not left alone.

2. You are in the left hand lane of a busy motorway. Signs indicate that your lane is closed 800 yards ahead. You should

   a. Signal right and pull up and wait for someone to give way.
   b. Switch on your hazard warning lights and edge over to the lane on your right.
   c. Wait until you reach the obstruction, then move across to the right.
   d. Move over to the lane on your right as soon as it is safe to do so.

3. As a car driver which THREE lanes must you not use?

   a. Crawler lane.
   b. Bus lane at the times shown.
   c. Overtaking lane.
   d. Acceleration lane.
   e. Cycle lane.
   f. Tram lane.

4. You are driving at 60mph in good conditions. What would be your shortest stopping distance?

   a. 23 metres (75 feet).
   b. 36 metres (120 feet).
   c. 53 metres (175 feet).
   d. 73 metres (240 feet).

5. Your vehicle pulls to one side when braking. You should

   a. Change the tyres around.
   b. Consult your garage as soon as possible.
   c. Pump the pedal when braking.
   d. Use your handbrake at the same time.

6. **When may you use hazard warning lights?**

   a. To park alongside another vehicle.
   b. To park on double yellow lines.
   c. When you are being towed.
   d. When you have broken down.

7. **You may not sound your horn**

   a. Between 10pm and 6am in a built up area.
   b. At any time in a built up area.
   c. Between 11.30pm and 7am in a built up area.
   d. Between 11.30pm and 6am in a built up area.

8. **Which THREE are suitable restraints for a child under three years old?**

   a. A child seat.
   b. An adult holding a child.
   c. An adult seat belt.
   d. A lap belt.
   e. A harness.
   f. A baby carrier.

9. **According to the Highway Code, what do the letters MSM mean?**

   a. Mirror – signal – manoeuvre.
   b. Manoeuvre – signal – mirror.
   c. Mirror – speed – manoeuvre.
   d. Manoeuvre – speed – mirror.

10. **A properly adjusted head restraint will**

    a. Make you more comfortable.
    b. Help you avoid neck injury.
    c. Help you relax.
    d. Help you maintain your driving position.

11. **A vehicle has a flashing green light. What does this mean?**

    a. A doctor is answering an emergency call.
    b. The vehicle is slow moving.
    c. It is a motorway police patrol vehicle.
    d. A vehicle is carrying hazardous chemicals.

12. **As a new driver, how can you decrease the risk of accidents on a motorway?**

   a. By keeping up with the car in front.
   b. By never driving over 45mph.
   c. By driving only in the nearside lane.
   d. By taking further training.

13. **How can you tell when you are driving over black ice?**

   a. It is easier to brake.
   b. The noise from your tyres sounds louder.
   c. You can see black ice on the road.
   d. Your steering feels light.

14. **You are braking on a wet road. Your vehicle begins to skid. You do not have anti-lock brakes. What is the first thing you should do?**

   a. Quickly pull up the handbrake.
   b. Release the footbrake fully.
   c. Push harder on the brake pedal.
   d. Gently use the accelerator.

15. **You are in a line of traffic. The driver behind you is following very closely. What action should you take?**

   a. Slow down and gradually increase the gap between you and the vehicle in front.
   b. Ignore the following driver and continue to drive within the speed limit.
   c. Signal left and wave the following driver past.
   d. Move to a position just left of the roads' centre line.

16. **Which FOUR of these must be in good working order for your car to be roadworthy?**

   a. Temperature gauge.
   b. Speedometer.
   c. Windscreen washers.
   d. Windscreen wipers.
   e. Oil warning light.
   f. Horn.

17. **A driver can only read a car number plate at the required distance with glasses on. The glasses should be worn**

    a. All the time when driving.
    b. Only when driving long distances.
    c. Only when reversing.
    d. Only in poor visibility.

18. **You are turning left on a slippery road. The rear of your vehicle slides to the right. You should**

    a. Brake firmly and not turn the steering wheel.
    b. Steer carefully to the left.
    c. Steer carefully to the right.
    d. Brake firmly and steer to the left.

19. **What are THREE ways that drinking alcohol can affect driving?**

    a. It slows down your reactions.
    b. It reduces your co-ordination.
    c. It affects you judgement of speed.
    d. It reduces your confidence.

20. **You are about to go down a steep hill. To control the speed of your vehicle you should**

    a. Select a high gear and use your brakes carefully.
    b. Select a high gear and use your brakes firmly.
    c. Select a low gear and use your brakes carefully.
    d. Select a low gear and avoid using your brakes.

21. **Where can you most likely to be affected by a cross wind?**

    a. On a narrow country lane.
    b. On an open stretch of road.
    c. On a busy stretch of road.
    d. On a long straight road.

22. **You are taking drugs which are likely to affect your driving. What should you do?**

    a. Seek medical advice before driving.
    b. Limit your driving to essential journeys.
    c. Only drive if accompanied by a full licence holder.
    d. Drive only for short distances.

23. At night you see a pedestrian who is wearing reflective clothing and carrying a bright red light. What does this mean?

    a. You are approaching road works.
    b. You are approaching an organised march.
    c. You are approaching a slow moving vehicle.
    d. You are approaching an accident black spot.

24. When driving a car fitted with automatic transmission, what would you use 'kick down' for?

    a. Cruise control.
    b. Quick acceleration.
    c. Slow braking.
    d. Fuel economy.

25. You could use the 'two second rule'

    a. Before restarting the engine after it has stalled.
    b. To keep a safe gap behind the vehicle in front.
    c. Before using the 'mirror-signal-manoeuvre' routine.
    d. When emerging on wet roads.

26. Your reactions will be much slower when driving

    a. If tired.
    b. In fog.
    c. Too quickly.
    d. In rain.

27. The minimum legal depth of tread for car tyres over three quarters of the breadth is

    a. 2.5mm.
    b. 4mm.
    c. 1mm.
    d. 1.6mm.

28. What is the main reason why your stopping distance is longer after heavy rain?

    a. You may not be able to see large puddles.
    b. The brakes will be cold because they are wet.
    c. Your tyres will have less grip on the road.
    d. Water on the windscreen will blur your view of the road.

29. **What is the most important factor in avoiding running into the car in front?**

   a.   Making sure your brakes are efficient.
   b.   Always driving at a steady speed.
   c.   Keeping the correct separation distance.
   d.   Having tyres which meet the legal requirements.

30. **It is very windy. You are about to overtake a motorcyclist. You should**

   a.   Overtake slowly.
   b.   Allow extra room.
   c.   Sound your horn.
   d.   Keep close as you pass.

31. **Which THREE result from drinking alcohol and driving?**

   a.   Less control.
   b.   A false sense of confidence.
   c.   Faster reactions.
   d.   Poor judgement of speed.
   e.   Greater awareness of danger.

32. **You wish to park facing downhill. Which TWO of the following should you do?**

   a.   Turn the steering wheel towards the kerb.
   b.   Park close to the bumper of another car.
   c.   Park with two wheels on the kerb.
   d.   Put the handbrake on firmly.
   e.   Turn the steering wheel away from the kerb.

33. **You are following a vehicle at a safe distance on a wet road. Another driver overtakes you and pulls into the gap you have left. What should you do?**

   a.   Flash your headlights as a warning.
   b.   Try to overtake safely as soon as you can.
   c.   Drop back to regain a safe distance.
   d.   Stay close to the other vehicle until it moves on.

34. **Skidding is mainly caused by**

   a.   The weather.
   b.   The driver.
   c.   The vehicle.
   d.   The road.

35. Which THREE does the law require you to keep in good condition?

    a. Gears.
    b. Clutch.
    c. Headlights.
    d. Windscreen.
    e. Seat belts.

36. You are towing a small trailer on a busy three lane motorway. All the lanes are open. You must (TWO answers)

    a. Not exceed 60mph.
    b. Not overtake.
    c. Have a stabiliser fitted.
    d. Use only the left and centre lanes.

37. Would it be safe to allow children to sit behind the rear seats of a hatchback car?

    a. Yes, if you can see clearly to the rear.
    b. Yes, if they are under 11 years of age.
    c. No, unless all the other seats are full.
    d. No, not in any circumstances.

38. You are first to arrive at the scene of an accident. Which FOUR of these should you do?

    a. Leave as soon as another motorist arrives.
    b. Switch off the vehicle's engine.
    c. Move uninjured people away from the vehicle.
    d. Call the emergency services.
    e. Warn other traffic.

39. You may make a 'U' turn

    a. When it is safe on a wide road.
    b. On a motorway when it is safe.
    c. In a wide one way street.
    d. By mounting both pavements carefully.

40. How should you use an emergency telephone on a motorway?

    a. Stay close to the carriageway.
    b. Face the oncoming traffic.
    c. Keep your back to the traffic.
    d. Keep your head in the kiosk.

41. You are in an accident on an 'A' class road. You have a warning triangle with you. At what distance before the obstruction should you place the warning triangle?

    a. 100 metres. (330 feet).
    b. 50 metres. (165 feet).
    c. 25 metres. (80 feet).
    d. 150 metres. (492 feet).

42. When should you switch on your hazard warning lights?

    a. When you cannot avoid causing an obstruction.
    b. When you are driving slowly due to bad weather.
    c. When you are towing a broken down vehicle.
    d. When you are parked on double yellow lines.

43. You are travelling at night. You are dazzled by headlights coming towards you. You should

    a. Pull down your sun visor.
    b. Slow down or stop.
    c. Switch on your main beam headlights.
    d. Put your hand over your eyes.

44. For what reason may you use the right hand lane of a motorway?

    a. For keeping out of the way of lorries.
    b. For driving at more than 70mph.
    c. For turning right.
    d. For overtaking other vehicles.

45. What is the national speed limit for cars and motorcycles in the centre lane of a three lane motorway?

    a. 40mph.
    b. 50mph.
    c. 60mph.
    d. 70mph.

46. You must not reverse

    a. For longer than necessary.
    b. For more than the length of a car.
    c. Into a side road.
    d. In a built up area.

47. Motorcyclists ride in daylight with their headlights switched on because

    a. It is a legal requirement.
    b. There is a speed trap ahead.
    c. They need to be seen.
    d. There are speed humps ahead.

48. Which THREE are likely to make you lose concentration whilst driving?

    a. Looking at road maps.
    b. Listening to loud music.
    c. Using your windscreen washers.
    d. Looking in your wing mirrors.
    e. Using a mobile phone.

49. You are reversing your vehicle into a side road. When would the greatest hazard to passing traffic occur?

    a. After you have completed the manoeuvre.
    b. Just before you actually begin the manoeuvre.
    c. After you have entered the side road.
    d. When the front of your vehicle swings out.

50. Where can you find reflective amber studs on a motorway?

    a. Separating the slip road from the carriageway.
    b. On the left hand edge of the road.
    c. On the right hand edge of the road.
    d. Separating the lanes.

ANSWERS QUESTION BANK – D

1abe 2d 3bef 4c 5b 6d 7c 8aef 9a 10b 11a 12d 13d 14b

15a 16bcdf 17a 18c 19abc 20c 21b 22a 23b 24b 25b 26a

27d 28c 29c 30b 31abd 32ad 33c 34b 35cde 36ad 37d

38bcde 39a 40b 41b 42a 43b 44d 45d 46a 47c 48abe 49d

50c

1. **You are testing your suspension. You notice that your vehicle keeps on bouncing when you press down on the front wing. What does this mean?**

   a. Worn tyres.
   b. Tyres are under inflated.
   c. Steering wheel is not located centrally.
   d. Worn shock absorbers.

2. **You are driving in slow moving queues of traffic. Before changing lane you should**

   a. Sound your horn.
   b. Look for motorcycles filtering through the traffic.
   c. Give a 'slowing down' arm signal.
   d. Change down to first gear.

3. **You think that the driver of the vehicle in front has forgotten to cancel his right indicator. You should**

   a. Sound your horn before overtaking.
   b. Overtake on the left if there is room.
   c. Flash your lights to alert the driver.
   d. Stay behind and not overtake.

4. **Excessive or uneven tyre wear can be caused by faults in the (TWO answers)**

   a. Braking system.
   b. Suspension.
   c. Gearbox.
   d. Exhaust system.

5. **The maximum prison sentence for the offence of driving whilst unfit through drink or drugs is**

   a. 12 months.
   b. 18 months.
   c. 6 months.
   d. 24 months.

6. Hazard warning lights should be used when vehicles are

    a. Broken down and causing an obstruction.
    b. Faulty and moving slowly.
    c. Being towed along the road.
    d. Reversing into a side road.

7. What is the braking distance at 50mph?

    a. 55 metres (180 feet).
    b. 24 metres (79 feet).
    c. 14 metres (45 feet).
    d. 38 metres (125 feet).

8. A pelican crossing which crosses the road in a straight line and has a central island must be treated as

    a. One crossing in daylight only.
    b. One complete crossing.
    c. Two separate crossings.
    d. Two crossings during darkness.

9. You are driving in heavy rain when your steering suddenly becomes very light. To get control again you must

    a. Brake firmly to reduce speed.
    b. Ease off the accelerator.
    c. Use the accelerator gently.
    d. Steer towards a dry part of the road.

10. Whilst driving along you meet a group of horses and riders from a riding school. Why should you be extra cautious?

    a. They will be moving in single file.
    b. They will be moving slowly.
    c. Many of the riders may be learners.
    d. The horses will panic more because they are in a group.

11. You are driving on an icy road. How can you avoid wheel spin?

    a. Drive at a slow speed in as high a gear as possible.
    b. Use the handbrake if the wheels start to spin.
    c. Brake gently and repeatedly.
    d. Drive in a low gear at all times.

12. It is important to wear suitable shoes when driving. Why is this?

    a. To prevent wear on the pedals.
    b. To maintain control of the pedals.
    c. To enable you to adjust your seat properly.
    d. To enable you to walk for assistance if you break down.

13. You are about to drive home, but cannot find the glasses you need to wear when driving. You should

    a. Drive home slowly, keeping to quiet roads.
    b. Borrow a friend's glasses and drive home.
    c. Drive home at night so that the lights will help you.
    d. Find a way of getting home without driving.

14. In very hot weather the road surface can get soft. Which TWO of the following will be affected most?

    a. The suspension.
    b. The steering.
    c. Braking.
    d. The windscreen.

15. You park overnight on a road with a 40mph speed limit. You should

    a. Park facing the traffic.
    b. Park with side lights on.
    c. Park with dipped headlights on.
    d. Park near a street light.

16. Where should you take particular care to look out for motorcyclists and cyclists?

    a. On dual carriageways.
    b. At junctions.
    c. At zebra crossings.
    d. On one-way streets.

17. When are you allowed to exceed the maximum speed limit?

    a. Between midnight and 6am.
    b. Never.
    c. When overtaking.
    d. When the road is clear.

18. Any load which is carried on a roof rack must be

    a. Securely fastened when driving.
    b. Carried only when strictly necessary.
    c. As light as possible.
    d. Covered with plastic sheeting.

19. In daylight an approaching motorcyclist is using a dipped headlight. Why?

    a. So that the rider can be seen more easily.
    b. To stop the battery overcharging.
    c. To improve the riders' vision.
    d. The rider is inviting you to proceed.

20. At 'toucan' crossings (TWO answers)

    a. There is no flashing amber light.
    b. Cyclists are not permitted.
    c. There is a continuously flashing amber beacon.
    d. Pedestrians and cyclists may cross.
    e. You only stop if someone is waiting to cross.

21. You are driving on a motorway. By mistake you pass the exit you wanted to take. You should

    a. Carefully reverse on the hard shoulder.
    b. Carry on to the next exit.
    c. Carefully reverse in the left hand lane.
    d. Make a u-turn at the next gap in the central reservation.

22. You are driving on a two lane dual carriageway. For which TWO of the following would you use the right hand lane?

    a. Turning right.
    b. Normal driving.
    c. Driving at the minimum allowed speed.
    d. Constant high speed driving.
    e. Overtaking slower traffic.
    f. Mending punctures.

23. When approaching a hazard your first reaction should be to

    a. Use your footbrake.
    b. Change direction.
    c. Release the accelerator.
    d. Check the mirrors.

24. **You are at a junction with limited visibility. You should**

    a. Inch forward looking to the right.
    b. Inch forward looking to the left.
    c. Inch forward looking both ways.
    d. Be ready to move off quickly.

25. **A long heavily loaded lorry is taking a long time to overtake. What should you do?**

    a. Speed up.
    b. Slow down.
    c. Hold your speed.
    d. Change direction.

26. **What is meant by 'defensive driving'?**

    a. Being alert and thinking ahead.
    b. Always driving slowly and gently.
    c. Always letting others go first.
    d. Pulling over for faster traffic.

27. **You are driving on a motorway. The car ahead shows its hazard lights for a short time. This tells you**

    a. The driver wants you to overtake.
    b. The other car is going to change lanes.
    c. Traffic ahead is slowing or stopping suddenly.
    d. There is a police speed check up ahead.

28. **You are on a road which is only wide enough for one vehicle. There is a car coming towards you. Which TWO of these would be correct?**

    a. Pull into a passing place on your right.
    b. Force the other driver to reverse.
    c. Pull into a any passing place if your vehicle is wider.
    d. Pull into a passing place on your left.
    e. Wait opposite a passing place on your right.
    f. Wait opposite a passing place on your left.

29. **You are driving along a road which has no traffic signs. There are street lights. What is the speed limit?**

    a. 20mph.
    b. 30mph.
    c. 40mph.
    d. 60mph.

30. Who has priority on unmarked crossroads?

    a. The driver of the larger vehicle.
    b. Nobody.
    c. The driver who is going fastest.
    d. The driver on the wider road.

31. You are leaving your vehicle parked on a road. When may you leave the engine running?

    a. If you will be parked for less than five minutes.
    b. If the battery is flat.
    c. If there is a passenger in the vehicle.
    d. Not on any occasion.

32. What is the right hand lane used for on a three lane motorway?

    a. Emergency vehicles only.
    b. Overtaking.
    c. Vehicles towing trailers.
    d. Coaches only.

33. In which of these situations would you avoid overtaking?

    a. Just after a bend.
    b. In a one-way street.
    c. On a 30mph road.
    d. Approaching a dip in the road.

34. When you are not sure whether it is safe to reverse your vehicle you should

    a. Use your horn.
    b. Rev your engine.
    c. Get out and check.
    d. Reverse slowly.

35. For which TWO of these must you show your insurance certificate?

    a. When you are taking your driving test.
    b. When buying or selling a vehicle.
    c. When a police officer asks you for it.
    d. When you are taxing your vehicle.
    e. When having an M.O.T. inspection.

36. When going straight ahead at a roundabout you should

    a. Indicate left before leaving the roundabout.
    b. Not indicate at any time.
    c. Indicate right when approaching the roundabout.
    d. Indicate left when approaching the roundabout.

37. What is the nearest you may park your vehicle to a junction?

    a. 10 metres (33 feet).
    b. 12 metres (40 feet).
    c. 15 metres (50 feet).
    d. 20 metres (65 feet).

38. You are parked on a busy high street. What is the safest way to turn your vehicle around to go in the opposite direction?

    a. Find a quiet side road to turn round in.
    b. Drive into a side road and reverse into the main road.
    c. Get someone to stop the traffic.
    d. Perform a 'U' turn.

39. To be able to drive you must be able to read a number plate from what distance?

    a. 10 metres (33 feet).
    b. 15 metres (50 feet).
    c. 20.5 metres (67 feet).
    d. 205 metres (673 feet).

40. You are driving on an icy road. What distance should you drive from the car in front?

    a. Eight times the normal distance.
    b. Six times the normal distance.
    c. Ten times the normal distance.
    d. Four times the normal distance.

41. On a motorway you may only stop on the hard shoulder

    a. In an emergency.
    b. If you feel tired and need to rest.
    c. If you miss the exit you wanted to take.
    d. To pick up a hitchhiker.

42. When may you use hazard warning lights whilst driving?

   a. Instead of sounding the horn in a built up area between 11.30pm and 7.00am.
   b. On a motorway or unrestricted dual carriageway to warn of a hazard ahead.
   c. On rural routes after a warning sign of animals.
   d. On the approach to toucan crossings where cyclists are waiting to cross.

43. Which of the following can travel on a motorway?

   a. Cyclists.
   b. Vans.
   c. Farm tractors.
   d. Learner drivers.

44. What type of emergency vehicle is fitted with a green light?

   a. Fire engine.
   b. Road gritter.
   c. Ambulance.
   d. Doctor's car.

45. After driving through a flood what is the first thing you should do?

   a. Stop and check the tyres.
   b. Stop and dry the brakes.
   c. Switch on your windscreen wipers.
   d. Test your brakes.

46. There are no speed limit signs on the road. How is a 30mph limit indicated?

   a. By hazard warning lines.
   b. By street lighting.
   c. By pedestrian islands.
   d. By double or single yellow lines.

47. You are travelling on a motorway. What colour are the reflective studs on the left of the carriageway?

   a. Green.
   b. Red.
   c. White.
   d. Amber.

48. Your vehicle has a puncture on a motorway. What should you do?

    a. Drive slowly to the next service area to get assistance.
    b. Pull up on the hard shoulder and change the wheel as quickly as possible.
    c. Pull up on the hard shoulder and use the emergency telephone to get assistance.
    d. Stop in your lane and switch on your hazard warning lights.

49. You are driving at night with full beam headlights on. A vehicle is overtaking you. You should dip your lights

    a. Some time after the vehicle has passed you.
    b. Before the vehicle starts to pass.
    c. Only if the other driver dips his headlights.
    d. As soon as the vehicle passes you.

50. An M.O.T. certificate is normally valid for

    a. Three years after the date it was issued.
    b. 10,000 miles.
    c. One year after the date it was issued.
    d. 30,000 miles.

ANSWERS QUESTION BANK – E

1d 2b 3d 4ab 5c 6a 7d 8b 9b 10c 11a 12b 13d 14bc 15b

16b 17b 18a 19a 20ad 21b 22ae 23d 24c 25b 26a 27c 28de

29b 30b 31d 32b 33d 34c 35cd 36a 37a 38a 39c 40c 41a

42b 43b 44d 45d 46b 47b 48c 49d 50c

1. **You are driving on a motorway. A large box falls onto the carriageway from a lorry ahead of you. The lorry does not stop. You should**

   a. Drive to the next emergency telephone and inform the police.
   b. Catch up with the lorry and try to get the drivers' attention.
   c. Stop close to the box and switch on your hazard warning lights until the police arrive.
   d. Pull over onto the hard shoulder and try to remove the box.

2. **A horse rider is in the left hand lane approaching a roundabout. A driver behind should expect the rider to**

   a. Go in any direction.
   b. Turn right.
   c. Turn left.
   d. Go ahead.

3. **You are driving on a motorway at night. You must have your headlights on unless**

   a. There are vehicles close in front of you.
   b. You are travelling below 50mph.
   c. The motorway is lit.
   d. Your vehicle is broken down on the hard shoulder.

4. **The main cause of brake fade is**

   a. The brakes overheating.
   b. Air in the brake fluid.
   c. Oil on the brakes.
   d. Brakes out of adjustment.

5. **When driving in fog in daylight you should use**

   a. Sidelights.
   b. Full beam headlights.
   c. Hazard lights.
   d. Dipped headlights.

6. **When may you sound the horn on your vehicle?**

   a. To give you right of way.
   b. To attract a friends' attention.
   c. To warn other drivers of your presence.
   d. To make slower drivers move over.

7. You are joining a motorway. Why is it important to make full use of the slip road?

   a. Because there is space available to reverse if you need to do so.
   b. To allow you direct access to the overtaking lanes.
   c. To build up speed similar to traffic on the motorway.
   d. Because you can continue on the hard shoulder.

8. What is the national speed limit on a single carriageway for cars and motorcycles?

   a. 70mph.
   b. 60mph.
   c. 50mph.
   d. 30mph.

9. You are driving at night and dazzled by the headlights of an oncoming car. You should

   a. Slow down or stop.
   b. Close your eyes.
   c. Flash your headlights.
   d. Pull down the sun visor.

10. You are driving on a motorway. You feel tired. You should

    a. Carry on, but drive slowly.
    b. Leave the motorway at the next exit.
    c. Complete your journey as quickly as possible.
    d. Stop on the hard shoulder.

11. You are driving on a motorway in windy conditions. When passing high-sided vehicles you should

    a. Increase your speed.
    b. Be wary of a sudden gust.
    c. Drive alongside very closely.
    d. Expect normal conditions.

12. You are driving on a main road. You intend to turn right into a side road. Just before turning you should

    a. Adjust your interior mirror.
    b. Flash your headlights.
    c. Steer over to the left.
    d. Check for traffic overtaking on your offside.

13. What is the national speed limit on motorways for cars and motorcycles?

   a. 30mph.
   b. 50mph.
   c. 60mph.
   d. 70mph.

14. Which of these is not allowed to travel in the right hand lane of a three lane motorway?

   a. A small delivery van.
   b. A motorcycle.
   c. A vehicle towing a trailer.
   d. A motorcycle and sidecar.

15. You wish to overtake a long slow-moving vehicle on a busy road. You should

   a. Wait behind until the driver waves you past.
   b. Flash your headlights for oncoming traffic to give way.
   c. Follow closely whilst moving out to see the road ahead.
   d. Keep well back until you can see that it is clear.

16. What is the safest way to brake?

   a. Brake lightly, then harder as you begin to stop, and then ease off just before stopping.
   b. Brake hard, put the gear lever into neutral and pull the handbrake on just before stopping.
   c. Brake lightly, push the clutch pedal down and pull the handbrake on just before stopping.
   d. Put the gear into neutral, brake hard and then ease off just before stopping.

17. Which THREE of these emergency services might have blue flashing beacons?

   a. Coastguard.
   b. Bomb disposal team.
   c. Gritting lorries.
   d. Animal ambulance.
   e. Mountain rescue.
   f. Doctors' cars.

18. Why is it particularly important to carry out a check on your vehicle before making a long motorway journey?

    a. You will have to carry out more harsh braking on motorways.
    b. Motorway service stations do not deal with breakdowns.
    c. The road surface will wear down the tyres faster.
    d. Continuous high speeds increase the risk of breakdowns.

19. Immediately after joining a motorway you should normally

    a. Try to overtake.
    b. Re-adjust your mirrors.
    c. Position your vehicle in the centre lane.
    d. Keep in the left lane.

20. Which TWO things would help to keep you alert during a long journey?

    a. Finishing your journey as fast as you can.
    b. Keeping off motorways and using country roads.
    c. Making sure that you get plenty of fresh air.
    d. Making regular stops for refreshments.

21. Which type of vehicle is most affected by strong winds?

    a. Tractor.
    b. Motorcycle.
    c. Car.
    d. Tanker.

22. You are travelling on a motorway at night with other vehicles just ahead of you. Which lights should you have on?

    a. Front fog lights.
    b. Main beam headlights.
    c. Sidelights only.
    d. Dipped headlights.

23. You are driving on a wet road. You have to stop your vehicle in an emergency. You should

    a. Apply the handbrake and footbrake together.
    b. Keep both hands on the wheel.
    c. Select reverse gear.
    d. Give an arm signal.

24. **At a crossroads there are no signs or road markings. Two vehicles approach. Who has priority?**

   a. Neither vehicle.
   b. The vehicle travelling the fastest.
   c. The vehicle on the widest road.
   d. Vehicles approaching from the right.

25. **Whilst driving you intend to turn left into a minor road. On the approach you should**

   a. Keep just left of the middle of the road.
   b. Keep in the middle of the road.
   c. Swing out wide just before turning.
   d. Keep well to the left of the road.

26. **What can cause heavy steering?**

   a. Driving on ice.
   b. Badly worn brakes.
   c. Over inflated tyres.
   d. Under inflated tyres.

27. **New petrol-engine cars must be fitted with catalytic converters. The reason for this is to**

   a. Control the exhaust noise levels.
   b. Prolong the life of the exhaust system.
   c. Allow the exhaust system to be recycled.
   d. Reduce harmful exhaust emissions.

28. **You are driving a slow moving vehicle on a narrow road. When traffic wishes to overtake you should**

   a. Take no action.
   b. Put your hazard warning lights on.
   c. Stop immediately and wave them on.
   d. Pull in safely as soon as you can do so.

29. **After a breakdown you need to rejoin the main carriageway of a motorway from the hard shoulder. You should**

   a. Move out onto the carriageway and then build up your speed.
   b. Move out onto the carriageway using your hazard lights.
   c. Gain speed on the hard shoulder before moving out onto the carriageway.
   d. Wait on the hard shoulder until someone flashes their headlights at you.

30. **You are on a narrow road at night. A slower moving vehicle ahead has been signalling right for some time. What should you do?**

    a. Overtake on the left.
    b. Flash your headlights before overtaking.
    c. Signal right and sound your horn.
    d. Wait for the signal to be cancelled before overtaking.

31. **You are driving towards a zebra crossing. Pedestrians are waiting to cross. You should**

    a. Give way to the elderly and infirm only.
    b. Slow down and prepare to stop.
    c. Use your headlights to indicate they can cross.
    d. Wave at them to cross the road.

32. **You get a puncture on the motorway. You manage to drive your vehicle onto the hard shoulder. You should**

    a. Change the wheel yourself immediately.
    b. Use the emergency telephone and call for assistance.
    c. Try to wave down another vehicle for help.
    d. Only change the wheel if you have a passenger to help.

33. **At night when leaving a motorway service area, you should**

    a. Drive for some time using only your side lights.
    b. Give your eyes time to adjust to the darkness.
    c. Switch on your interior light until your eyes adjust.
    d. Close your eyes for a moment before leaving the slip road.

34. **Why should your tyres be kept to the pressure the manufacturer tells you?**

    a. To keep the car the right height off the road.
    b. To save wear on the engine.
    c. To stop the car from sloping to one side.
    d. To help prevent the car from skidding.

35. **You are waiting at a level crossing. A train has passed, but the lights keep flashing. You must**

    a. Carry on waiting.
    b. Phone the signal operator.
    c. Edge over the stop line and look for trains.
    d. Park your vehicle and investigate.

36. Which of these, if allowed to get low, could cause an accident?

 a. Antifreeze level.
 b. Brake fluid level.
 c. Battery water level.
 d. Radiator coolant level.

37. To move off safely from a parked position you should

 a. Signal if other drivers will need to slow down.
 b. Not look round if there is vehicle parked close in front of you.
 c. Give a hand signal as well as using your indicators.
 d. Use your mirrors and look round for a final check.

38. The offence of causing death whilst driving under the influence of drink or drugs carries the maximum penalty of

 a. Eight years imprisonment.
 b. Ten years imprisonment.
 c. Twelve years imprisonment.
 d. Six years imprisonment.

39. Where on a motorway would you find green reflective studs?

 a. Separating driving lanes.
 b. Between the hard shoulder and the carriageway.
 c. At slip road entrances and exits.
 d. Between the carriageway and the central reservation.

40. The cost of your insurance may be reduced if

 a. Your car is large and powerful.
 b. You are using the car for work purposes.
 c. You have penalty points on your licence.
 d. You are over 25 years of age.

41. Your doctor has given you a course of medicine. Why should you ask if it is O.K. to drive?

 a. Drugs make you a better driver by quickening your reactions.
 b. You will have to let your insurance company know about the medicine.
 c. Some types of medicine can cause your reactions to slow down.
 d. The medicine you take will make you more alert.

42. You meet an obstruction on your side of the road. You must

    a. Drive on. It is your right of way.
    b. Give way to oncoming traffic.
    c. Wave oncoming vehicles through.
    d. Accelerate to get past first.

43. You are overtaking a car at night. You must be sure that

    a. You flash your headlights before overtaking.
    b. Your rear fog lights are switched on.
    c. You have switched your lights to full beam before overtaking.
    d. You do not dazzle other road users.

44. What is the national speed limit for cars and motorcycles on a dual carriageway?

    a. 30mph.
    b. 50 mph.
    c. 60mph.
    d. 70mph.

45. On a foggy day you unavoidably have to park your car on the road. You should

    a. Leave your headlights on.
    b. Leave your fog lights on.
    c. Leave your side lights on.
    d. Leave your hazard lights on.

46. On a motorway the reflective amber studs can be found between

    a. The hard shoulder and the carriageway.
    b. The acceleration lane and the carriageway.
    c. The central reservation and the carriageway.
    d. Each pair of lanes.

47. At which of these places are you sometimes allowed to park your vehicle?

    a. On the nearside lane of a motorway.
    b. On a clearway.
    c. Where there is a single broken yellow line.
    d. On the zigzag lines of a zebra crossing.

48. A basic rule when driving on motorways is

    a. Use the lane which has the least traffic.
    b. Keep to the left lane unless overtaking.
    c. Overtake on the side which is clearest.
    d. Try to keep above 50mph to avoid congestion.

49. You are driving at the legal speed limit. A vehicle behind wants to overtake. Should you try to prevent the driver from overtaking?

    a. No, unless it is safe to do so.
    b. Yes, because the other driver is acting dangerously.
    c. No, not at any time.
    d. Yes, because the other driver is breaking the law.

50. Your vehicle has broken down on a motorway. You are not able to stop on the hard shoulder. What should you do first?

    a. Switch on your hazard warning lights.
    b. Stop following traffic and ask for help.
    c. Attempt to repair your vehicle quickly.
    d. Place a warning triangle in the road.

ANSWERS QUESTION BANK – F

1a 2a 3d 4a 5d 6c 7c 8b 9a 10b 11b 12d 13d 14c 15d

16a 17ade 18d 19d 20cd 21b 22d 23b 24a 25d 26d 27d

28d 29c 30d 31b 32b 33b 34d 35a 36b 37d 38b 39c 40d

41c 42b 43d 44d 45b 46c 47c 48b 49c 50a

1. **It is illegal to drive with tyres that**

   a. Have a large deep cut in the side wall.
   b. Have been bought second hand.
   c. Are of different makes.
   d. Have painted walls.

2. **A bus is stopped at a bus stop ahead of you. Its' right hand indicator is flashing. You should**

   a. Flash your headlights and slow down.
   b. Slow down and give way if it is safe to do so.
   c. Sound your horn and keep going.
   d. Slow down and then sound your horn.

3. **When snow is falling heavily you should**

   a. Drive as long as your headlights are used.
   b. Not drive unless you have a mobile phone.
   c. Drive only when your journey is short.
   d. Not drive unless it's essential.

4. **Why is pressing the clutch pedal down for long periods a bad habit?**

   a. It reduces the cars' speed when going down hill.
   b. It causes the engine to wear out more quickly.
   c. It reduces the drivers' control of the vehicle.
   d. It causes the engine to use more fuel.

5. **You want to reverse into a side road. You are not sure whether the area behind you is clear. What should you do?**

   a. Look through the rear window only.
   b. Get out and check.
   c. Check the mirrors only.
   d. Carry on and assume it's clear.

6. **How often should you stop on a long journey?**

   a. When you need petrol.
   b. At least every four hours.
   c. At least every two hours.
   d. When you need to eat.

7. **Which vehicles are normally fitted with amber flashing lights?**
(TWO answers)

    a. Doctors' car.
    b. Bomb disposal team.
    c. Blood transfusion team.
    d. Breakdown recovery vehicles.
    e. Coastguard.
    f. Maintenance vehicles.

8. **Whilst driving you approach a large puddle which is close to the left hand kerb. Pedestrians are close to the water. You should**
(TWO answers)

    a. Ignore the puddle.
    b. Brake suddenly and sound your horn.
    c. Slow down before the puddle.
    d. Try to avoid splashing the pedestrians.
    e. Wave at the pedestrians to keep back.

9. **You want to turn right from a junction, your view is restricted by parked vehicles. What should you do?**

    a. Move out quickly, but be prepared to stop.
    b. Sound your horn and pull out if there is no reply.
    c. Stop. Then move slowly forward until you have a clear view.
    d. Stop. Get out and look along the main road to check.

10. **You are planning to drive a long distance. Which THREE things will make the journey safer?**

    a. Avoid travelling at night.
    b. Ensure a supply of fresh air.
    c. Avoid motorways.
    d. Make stops for refreshments.
    e. Drive slowly.

11. **Which of the following is a major cause of motorcycle collisions?**

    a. Car drivers.
    b. Moped riders.
    c. Sunny weather conditions.
    d. Traffic lights.

12. You should only flash your headlights to other road users

   a.   To show that you are giving way.
   b.   To show that you are about to give way.
   c.   To tell them that you have right of way.
   d.   To let them know that you are there.

13. How does alcohol affect your driving?

   a.   It speeds up your reactions.
   b.   It increases your awareness.
   c.   It improves your co-ordination.
   d.   It reduces your concentration.

14. There is a police car following you. The police officer flashes his headlights and points to the left. What should you do?

   a.   Turn at the next left.
   b.   Pull up on the left.
   c.   Stop immediately.
   d.   Move over to the left.

15. You should avoid 'coasting' your vehicle because it could

   a.   Damage the suspension.
   b.   Increase tyre wear.
   c.   Flatten the battery.
   d.   Reduce steering control.

16. When are you allowed to drive if your brake lights do not work?

   a.   During the daytime.
   b.   When going for an M.O.T. test.
   c.   At no time.
   d.   In an emergency.

17. When driving, what is the maximum legal level for alcohol in your blood?

   a.   50mg per 100ml.
   b.   60mg per 100ml.
   c.   80mg per 100ml.
   d.   90mg per 100ml.

18. You see a pedestrian with a white stick and two red reflective bands on it. It means that the person is

   a. Physically disabled.
   b. Deaf and speech impaired.
   c. Blind and speech impaired.
   d. Deaf and blind.

19. What advice do you give a driver who has had a few alcoholic drinks at a party?

   a. Have a strong cup of coffee and then drive home.
   b. Drive home carefully and slowly.
   c. Wait a short while and then drive home.
   d. Go home by public transport.

20. Following a large goods vehicle too closely is dangerous because

   a. Your field of vision is seriously reduced.
   b. Slipstreaming will reduce wind affect.
   c. Your engine will overheat.
   d. Your brakes need a constant cooling affect.

21. A vehicle pulls out in front of you at a junction. What should you do?

   a. Swerve past it and blow your horn.
   b. Flash your headlights and drive up close behind.
   c. Slow down and be ready to stop.
   d. Accelerate past it immediately.

22. You should only use a handheld telephone when

   a. Your vehicle has an automatic gear change.
   b. Driving at low speeds.
   c. You have stopped at a safe place.
   d. Travelling on minor roads.

23. To drive on the road learners must

   a. Have no penalty points on their licence.
   b. Have taken professional instruction.
   c. Have a signed and valid provisional licence.
   d. Apply for a driving test within 12 months.

24. How should you overtake horse riders?

   a. Drive up close and overtake as soon as possible.
   b. Speed is not important, but you should allow plenty of room.
   c. Use your horn just once to warn them.
   d. Drive slowly and allow plenty of room.

25. In which FOUR places must you not park or wait?

   a. On a dual carriageway.
   b. At or near a bus stop.
   c. On the slope of a hill.
   d. Opposite a traffic island.
   e. In front of someone's drive.
   f. On the brow of a hill.

26. You are intending to leave the motorway at the next exit. Before you reach the exit you should normally position your vehicle

   a. In the middle lane.
   b. In the left hand lane.
   c. On the hard shoulder.
   d. In any lane.

27. You are on a busy main road and find that you are travelling in the wrong direction. What should you do?

   a. Turn into a side road on the right and reverse into the main road.
   b. Make a 'U' turn in the main road.
   c. Make a 'three point turn' in the main road.
   d. Turn round in a side road.

28. Your vehicle has broken down on an automatic railway level crossing. What should you do first?

   a. Get everyone out of the vehicle and clear of the crossing.
   b. Phone the signal operator so that trains are stopped.
   c. Walk along the track to warn any approaching trains.
   d. Try to push the vehicle clear of the crossing as soon as possible.

29. Which one of the following is not affected by alcohol?

   a. Judgement of speed.
   b. Reaction time.
   c. Perception of colour.
   d. Co-ordination.

30. Motorcyclists will often look round over their right shoulder just before turning right. This is because

a. They need to listen for following traffic.
b. Motorcycles do not have mirrors.
c. Looking round helps them to balance as they turn.
d. They need to check for traffic in their blind area.

31. When emerging from a side road into a queue of traffic which vehicles can be especially hard to see?

a. Motorcycles.
b. Tractors.
c. Milk floats.
d. Cars.

32. You are coming up to a roundabout. A cyclist is signalling to turn right. What should you do?

a. Overtake on the right.
b. Give a horn warning.
c. Signal the cyclist to move across.
d. Give the cyclist plenty of room.

33. You can park on the right hand side of the road at night

a. In a one way street.
b. With your side lights on.
c. More than 10 metres (33 feet) from a junction.
d. Under a lamp post.

34. Where you see street lights but no speed limit signs the limit is usually

a. 30mph.
b. 40mph.
c. 50mph.
d. 60mph.

35. You are going along a single track road in a slow vehicle with passing places only on the right. The driver behind you wishes to overtake. You should

a. Speed up to get away from the following driver.
b. Switch on your hazard warning lights.
c. Wait opposite a passing place on your right.
d. Drive into a passing place on your right.

36. In which THREE places must you never park your vehicle?

   a. Near the brow of a hill.
   b. At or near a bus stop.
   c. Where there is no pavement.
   d. Within 10 metres (33 feet) of a junction.
   e. On a 40mph road.

37. What are TWO reasons why coasting downhill is wrong?

   a. Petrol consumption will be higher.
   b. The vehicle will pick up speed.
   c. It puts more wear and tear on the tyres.
   d. You have less braking and steering control.
   e. It damages the engine.

38. It is essential that tyre pressures are checked regularly. When should this be done?

   a. After any lengthy journey.
   b. After driving at high speed.
   c. When tyres are hot.
   d. When tyres are cold.

39. There is a slow moving motorcyclist ahead of you. You are unsure what the rider is going to do. You should

   a. Pass on the left.
   b. Pass on the right.
   c. Stay behind.
   d. Move closer.

40. Your vehicle has a puncture on a motorway. What should you do?

   a. Drive slowly to the next service area for assistance.
   b. Pull up on the hard shoulder and change the wheel as quickly as possible.
   c. Pull up on the hard shoulder and use the emergency telephone to get assistance.
   d. Switch on your hazard warning lights and stop in your lane.

41. Another driver's behaviour upsets you. It may help if you

   a. Stop and take a break.
   b. Shout abusive language.
   c. Gesture to them with your hand.
   d. Follow their car flashing your headlights.

42. A flashing green light on a vehicle means

    a. Police on non-urgent duties.
    b. Doctor on an emergency call.
    c. Road safety patrol operating.
    d. Gritting in progress.

43. What should you use horn for?

    a. To alert others to your presence.
    b. To claim your right of way.
    c. To greet other road users.
    d. To signal your annoyance.

44. When joining a motorway you must always

    a. Use the hard shoulder.
    b. Stop at the end of the acceleration lane.
    c. Come to a stop before joining the motorway.
    d. Give way to traffic already on the motorway.

45. You are the first person to arrive at an accident where people are badly injured. Which THREE things should you do?

    a. Switch on your own hazard warning lights.
    b. Make sure that someone phones for an ambulance.
    c. Try and get people who are injured to drink something.
    d. Move those who are injured clear of their vehicles.
    e. Get people who are not injured clear of the scene.

46. Which TWO are correct? The passing places on a single track road are

    a. For taking a rest from driving.
    b. To pull into if an oncoming vehicle wants to proceed.
    c. For stopping and checking your route.
    d. To turn the car around in if you are lost.
    e. To pull into if the car behind wants to overtake.

47. Which TWO of the following are correct? When overtaking at night you should

    a. Wait until a bend so that you can see the oncoming headlights.
    b. Sound your horn twice before moving out.
    c. Be careful because you can see less.
    d. Beware of bends in the road ahead.
    e. Put headlights on full beam.

48. **A rumble device is designed to** (TWO answers)

   a. Give directions.
   b. Prevent cattle escaping.
   c. Alert drivers to low tyre pressure.
   d. Alert drivers to a hazard.
   e. Encourage drivers to reduce speed.

49. **How can you stop a caravan from snaking from side to side?**

   a. Turn the steering wheel slowly to each side.
   b. Accelerate to increase your speed.
   c. Stop as quickly as you can.
   d. Slow down very gradually.

50. **As a provisional licence holder you should not drive your car**

   a. Over 50mph.
   b. At night.
   c. On a motorway.
   d. With passengers in the rear seats.

ANSWERS QUESTION BANK – G

1a 2b 3d 4c 5b 6c 7df 8cd 9c 10abd 11c 12d 13d 14b

15d 16c 17c 18d 19d 20a 21c 22c 23c 24d 25bdef 26b 27d

28a 29c 30d 31a 32d 33a 34a 35c 36abd 37bd 38d 39c 40c

41a 42b 43a 44d 45abe 46be 47cd 48de 49d 50c

THE LEARNER DRIVERS QUIZ BOOK

This book has been prepared to help 21st century learners pass their driving theory test first time. It follows closely the rules and regulations for safe driving as laid down by the Driving & Vehicle Standards Agency (DVSA). It contains 200 multiple choice questions, complete with answers, in ten banks of 20 questions each. The correct answers are shown at the end of each bank of questions.

THE LEARNER DRIVERS CLICK BOOK

This Ebook has been prepared to help 21st century learners pass their driving test first time. It has fully clickable content to help you navigate around all the lesson plans. It follows closely the requirements for learning to drive as laid down by the Driving & Vehicle Standards Agency (DVSA). In its various sections it includes twelve complete and fully colour illustrated lesson plans covering all the elements which can be tested by the DVSA; plus over 150 fully detailed colour illustrations.

THE LEARNER DRIVERS HANDBOOK

This handbook has been prepared to help learners pass their DVSA test first time. It follows closely the requirements for learning to drive as laid down by the Driving & Vehicle Standards Agency. In its various sections it includes twelve complete and fully colour illustrated lesson plans covering all the elements which can be tested. It also has over 150 fully detailed colour illustrations.

EASY LESSONS FOR LEARNER DRIVERS

A learner drivers version of the driving instructors Easy Lesson Plans book, complete with all the illustrations. The lessons are identical to the instructors' version to ensure that both are reading from the same script. It is tailored specifically to help learners pass their driving test and obtain a full driving licence.

WHAT DO YOU SEE?

A series of photographic real life road images with revealing texts designed to help learner drivers spot potential hazards and become more aware of their surroundings whilst driving. An excellent aid to developing awareness which may one day be remembered as time well spent by saving your life.

A THOUSAND AND ONE QUESTIONS FOR TRAINEE DRIVING INSTRUCTORS

Multiple choice questions complete with answers to help trainees through the A.D.I. theory test by encouraging them to research answers in recommended reading. It's an invaluable aid to passing the test first time and saving money on retest fees.

EASY LESSONS PLANS FOR DRIVING INSTRUCTORS & TRAINEE A.D.I.s

A fully colour illustrated training manual containing 12 lesson plans covering all the key subjects learner drivers need to be taught. In addition it has sections detailing the suggested correct phraseology when giving route directions, the most common faults committed by learner drivers and a guide to identify signs of nerves plus 18 blank typical road layouts which can be printed off and laminated for illustrating problems with a dry marker pen.

THE DRIVING INSTRUCTOR BUSINESS

An in depth insight into all aspects of what is actually the business of being an A.D.I. Dealing with such issues as how to get pupils, how to keep them, how to conduct lessons, what to charge, general finances and overheads, including the psychological and material benefits and much more.

ACKNOWLEDGEMENTS

The images of road traffic signs contained herein are Crown Copyright and are reproduced with the appropriate authority.

www.ingramcontent.com/pod-product-compliance
Lightning Source LLC
Chambersburg PA
CBHW021239280526
45784CB00005B/2158